HAL•LEONARD
INSTRUMENTAL
PLAY-ALONG

AUDIO
ACCESS
INCLUDED

CLARINET

JAMES BOND

T0066182

PLAYBACK+
Speed • Pitch • Balance • Loop

To access audio visit:
www.halleonard.com/mylibrary

Enter Code
5177-7722-2995-6561

Audio arrangements by Peter Deneff

ISBN 978-1-4950-6079-3

Music Sales America

EXCLUSIVELY DISTRIBUTED BY
HAL•LEONARD®
7777 W. BLUEMOUND RD. P.O. BOX 13819 MILWAUKEE, WI 53213

Visit Hal Leonard Online at
www.halleonard.com

DIAMONDS ARE FOREVER

from DIAMONDS ARE FOREVER

CLARINET

Words by DON BLACK
Music by JOHN BARRY

FOR YOUR EYES ONLY

from FOR YOUR EYES ONLY

CLARINET

Lyrics by MICHAEL LESSON
Music by BILL CONTI

FROM RUSSIA WITH LOVE

from FROM RUSSIA WITH LOVE

CLARINET

Words and Music by
LIONEL BART

GOLDFINGER

from GOLDFINGER

CLARINET

Music by JOHN BARRY
Lyrics by LESLIE BRICUSSE and ANTHONY NEWLEY

JAMES BOND THEME

CLARINET

By MONTY NORMAN

LIVE AND LET DIE

from LIVE AND LET DIE

CLARINET

Words and Music by PAUL McCARTNEY
and LINDA McCARTNEY

NOBODY DOES IT BETTER

from THE SPY WHO LOVED ME

CLARINET

Music by MARVIN HAMLISCH
Lyrics by CAROLE BAYER SAGER

ON HER MAJESTY'S SECRET SERVICE - THEME

CLARINET

By JOHN BARRY

SKYFALL

from the Motion Picture SKYFALL

CLARINET

Words and Music by ADELE ADKINS
and PAUL EPWORTH

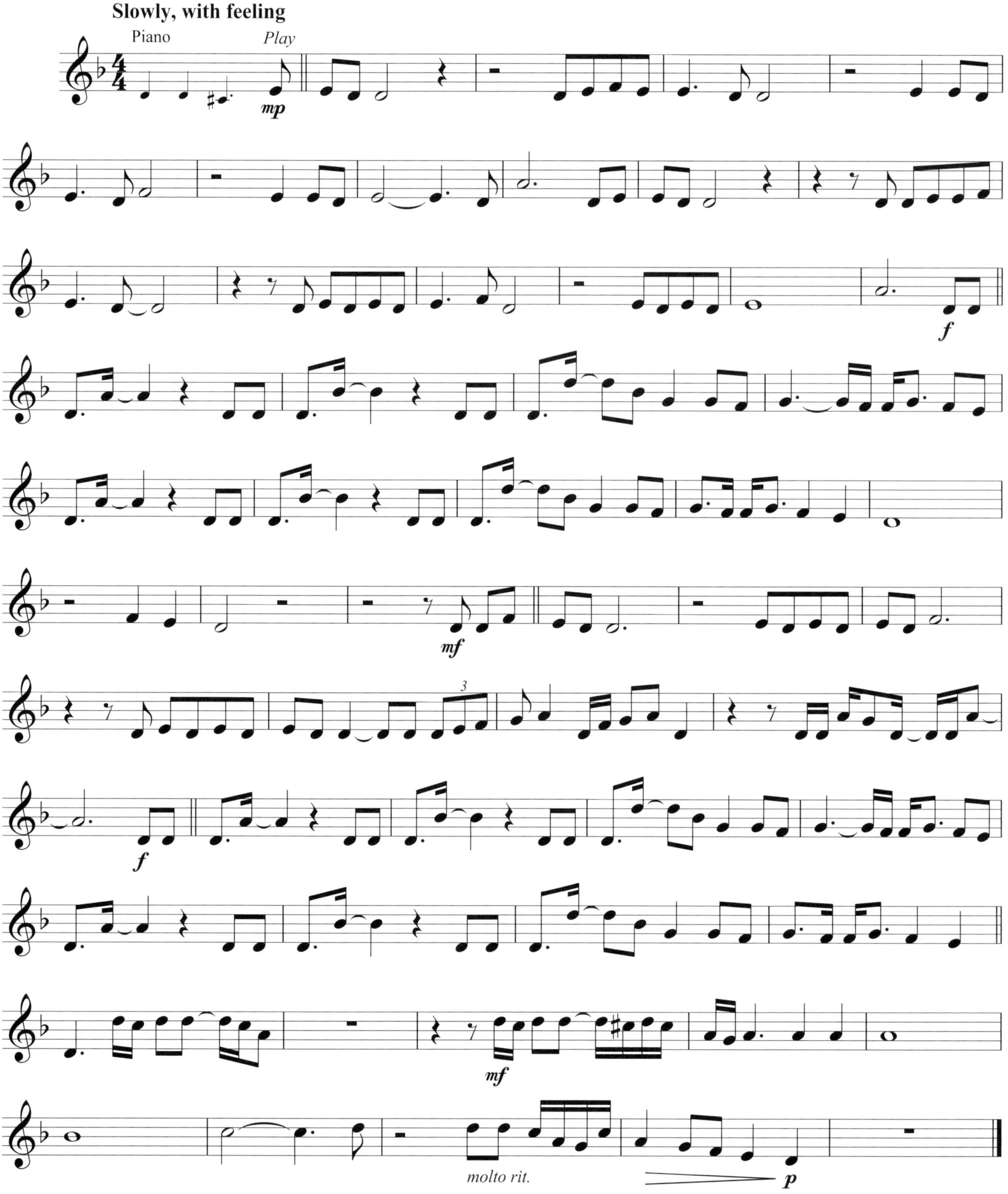

A VIEW TO A KILL

from A VIEW TO A KILL

CLARINET

Words and Music by JOHN BARRY
and DURAN DURAN

WRITING'S ON THE WALL

from the film SPECTRE

CLARINET

Words and Music by SAM SMITH
and JAMES NAPIER

YOU ONLY LIVE TWICE

from YOU ONLY LIVE TWICE

CLARINET

Music by JOHN BARRY
Lyrics by LESLIE BRICUSSE